I Love You, My Little Cub

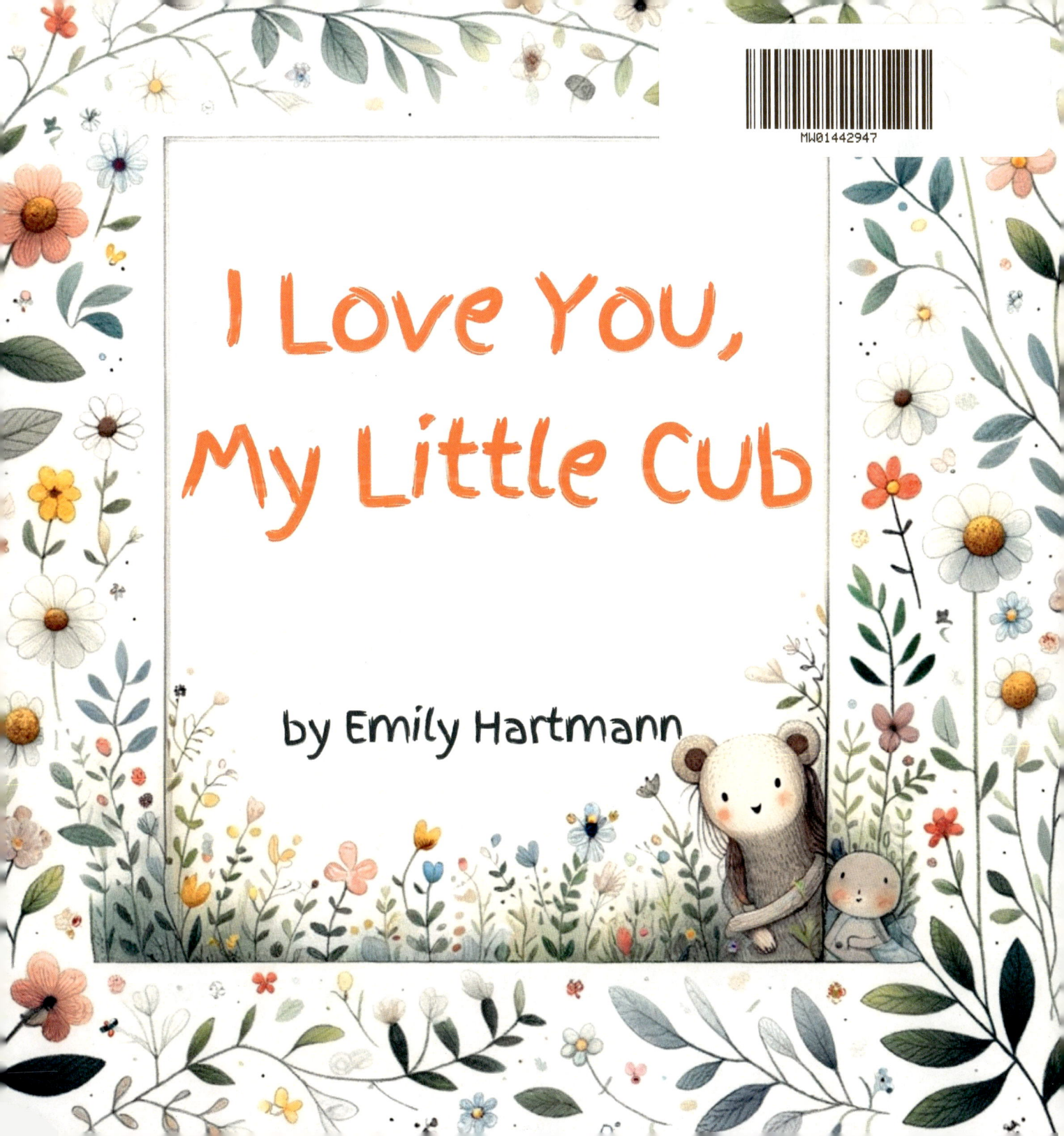

by Emily Hartmann

Copyright © 2023 by Emily Hartmann

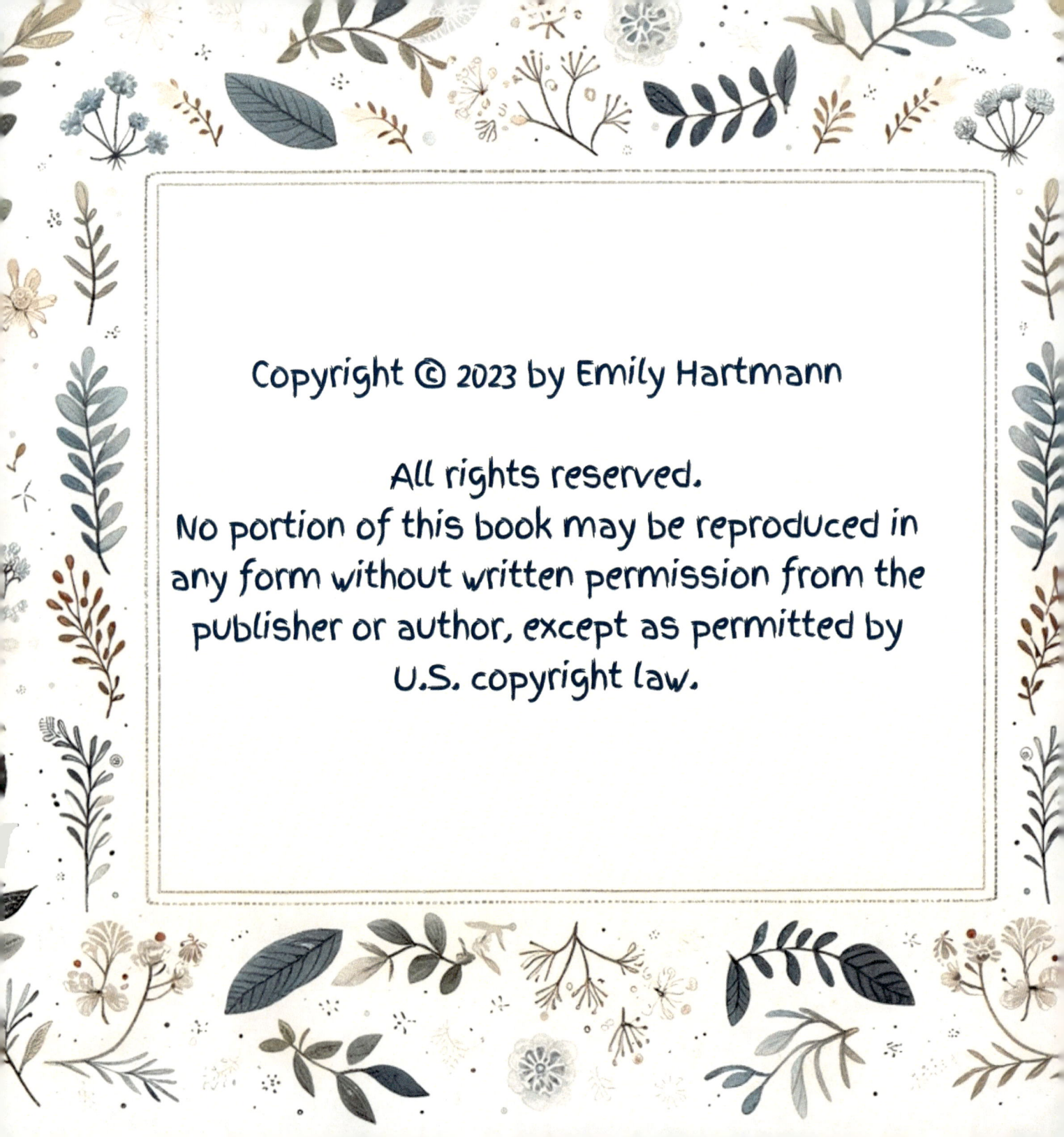

All rights reserved.
No portion of this book may be reproduced in any form without written permission from the publisher or author, except as permitted by U.S. copyright law.

GOOD NIGHT LITTLE FARM

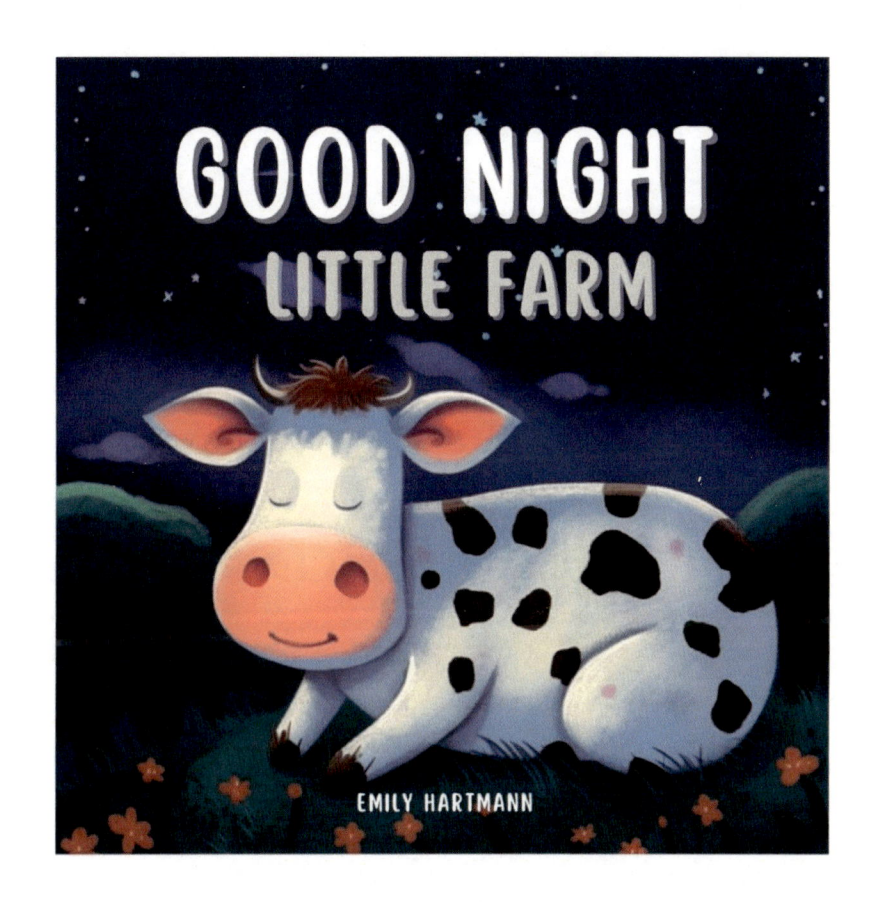

EMILY HARTMANN

CLICK HERE get your free copy

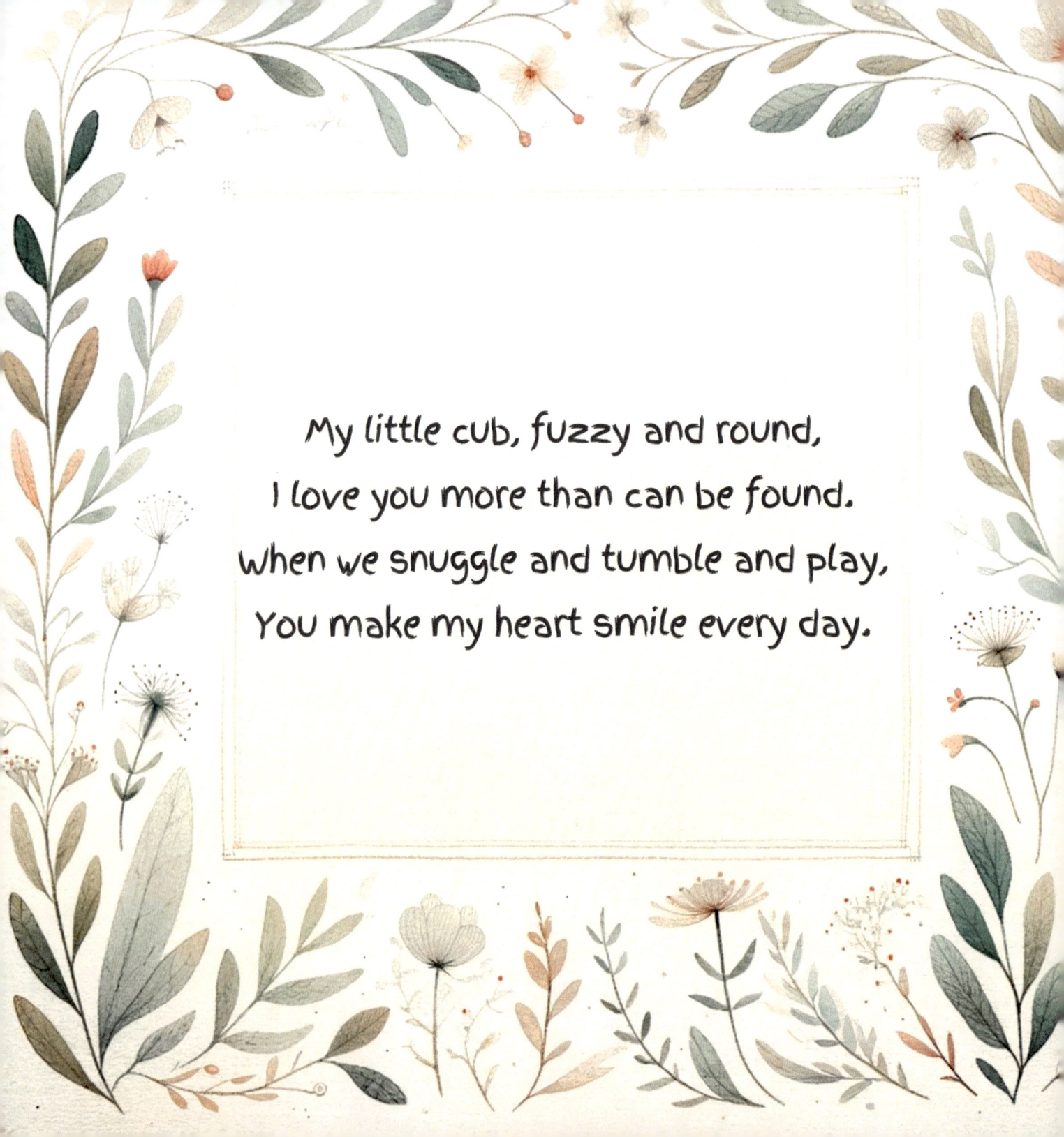

My little cub, fuzzy and round,
I love you more than can be found.
When we snuggle and tumble and play,
You make my heart smile every day.

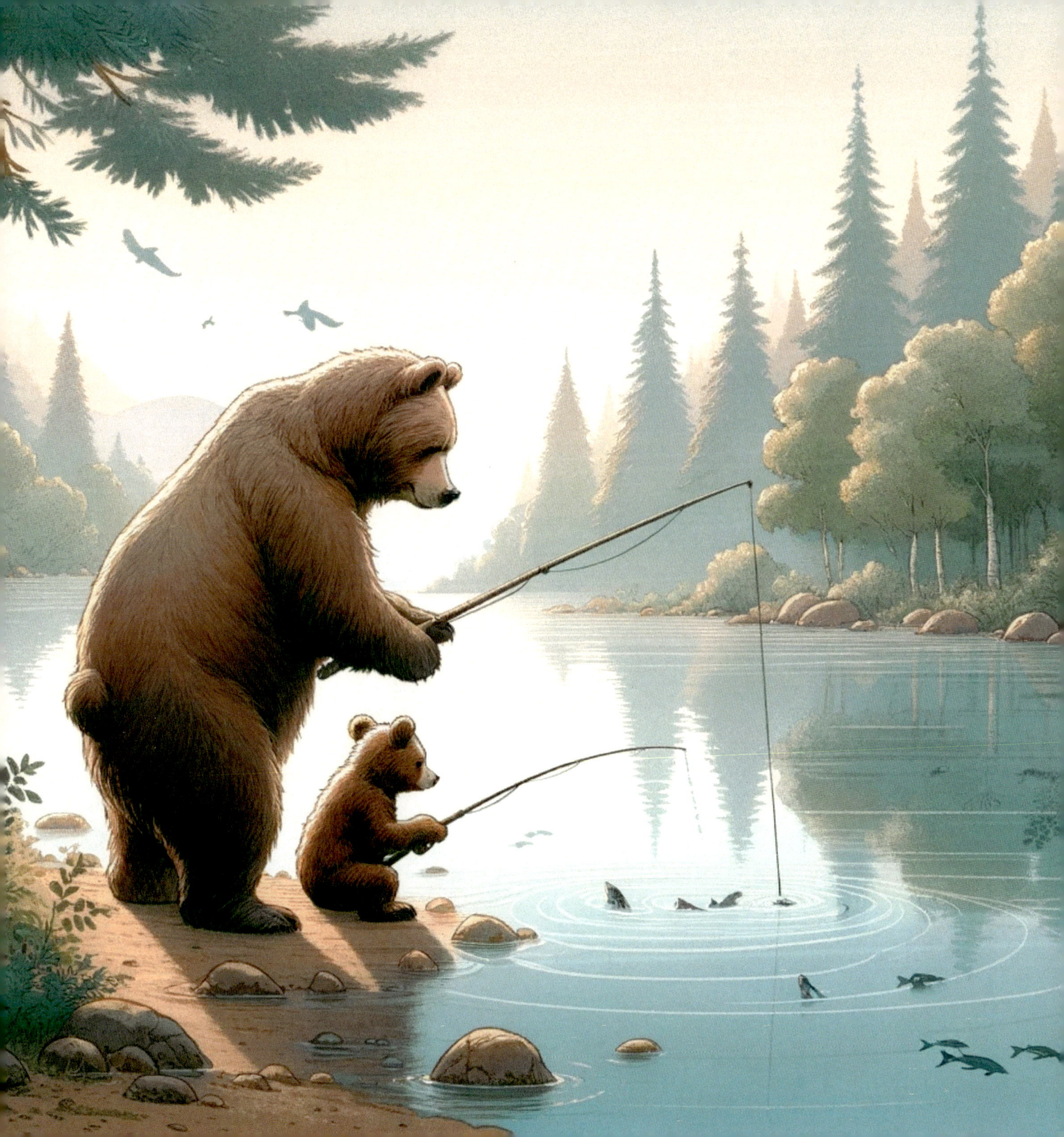

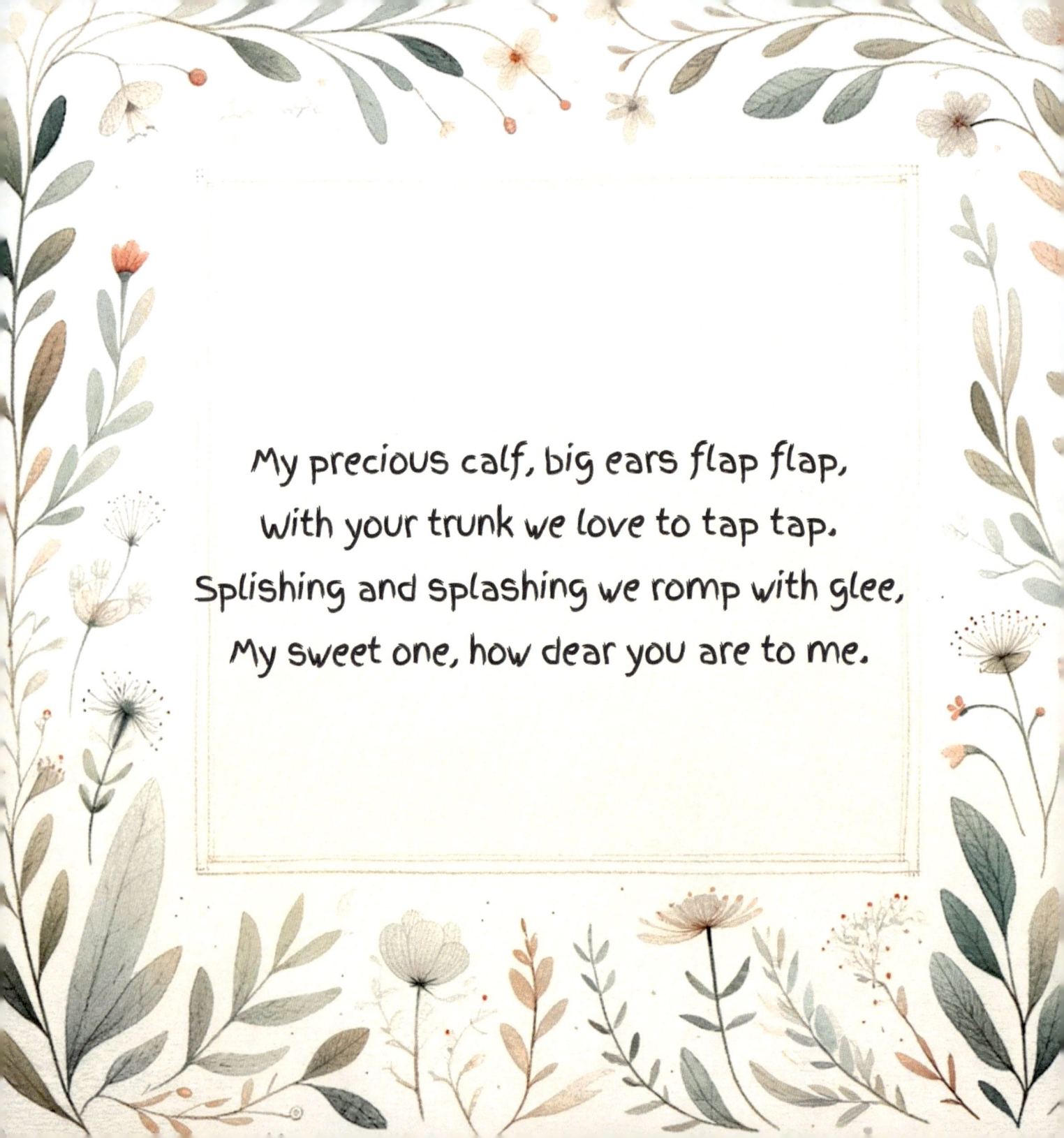

My precious calf, big ears flap flap,
with your trunk we love to tap tap.
Splishing and splashing we romp with glee,
My sweet one, how dear you are to me.

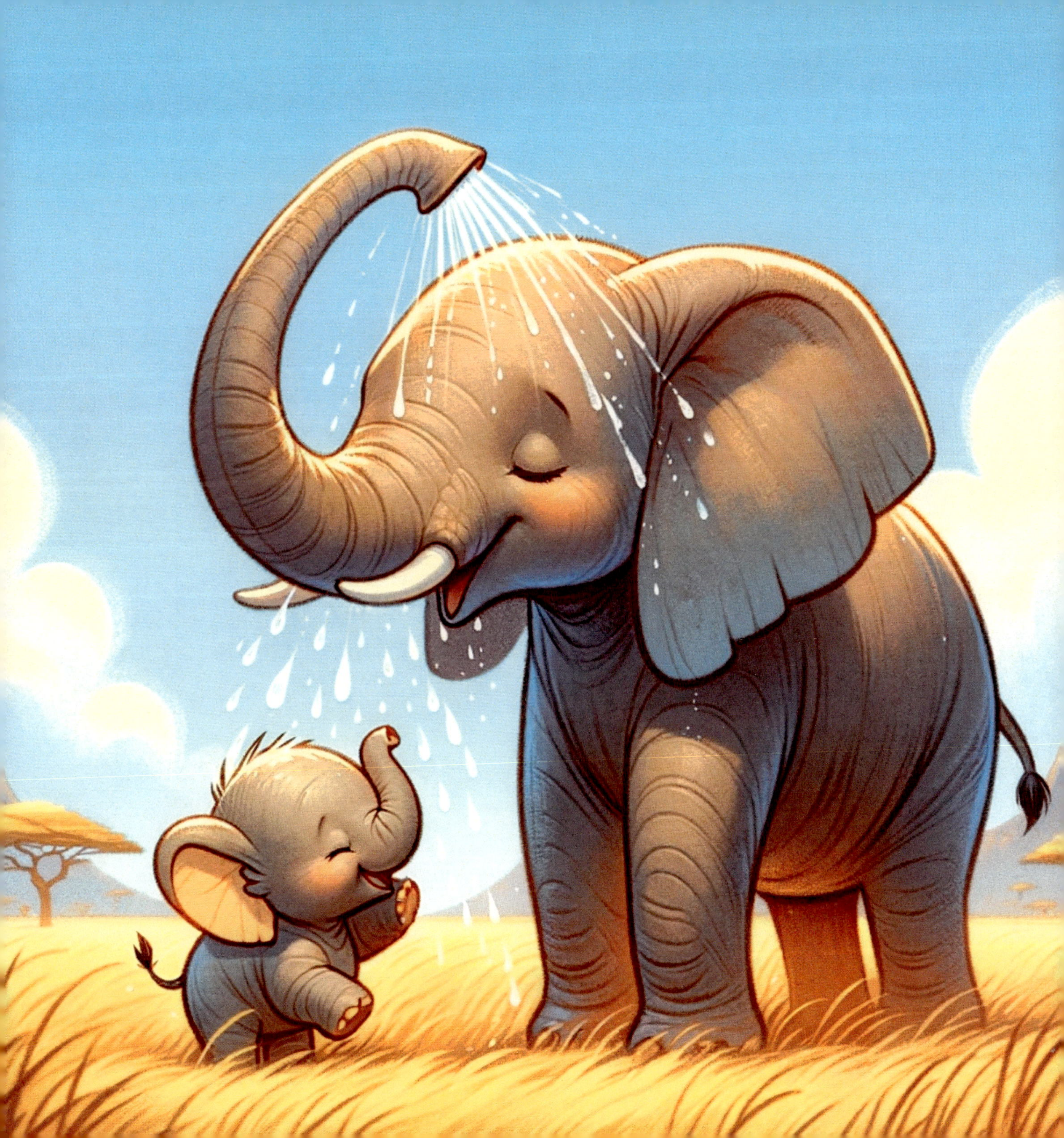

My leggy baby giraffe so tall,
I love you most of all.
Munching leaves high up in trees,
You fill my heart with joy and ease.

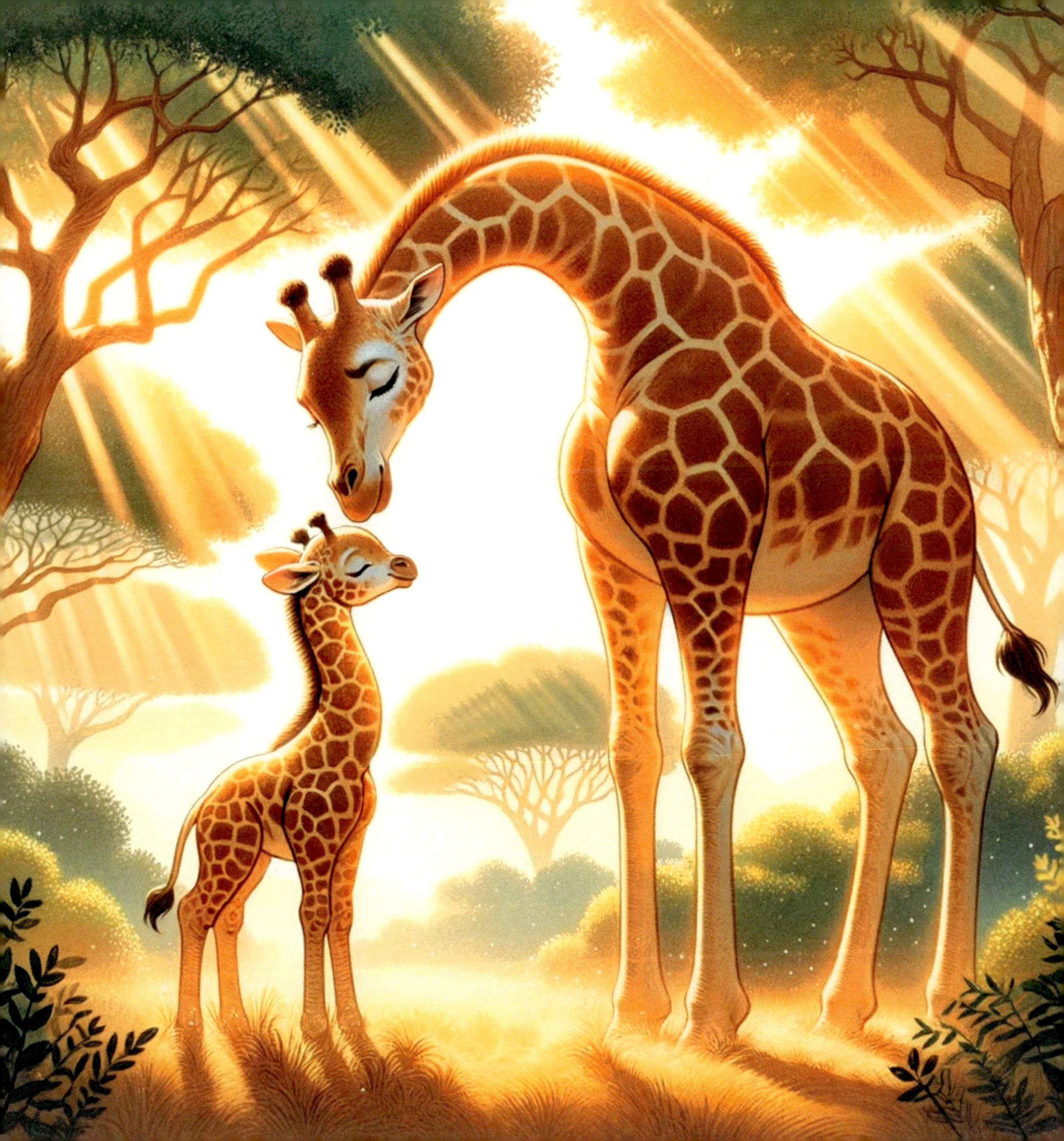

My owlet, with eyes so bright,
You are my moonlight.
As we swoop and hoot and glide at night,
You make everything feel just right.

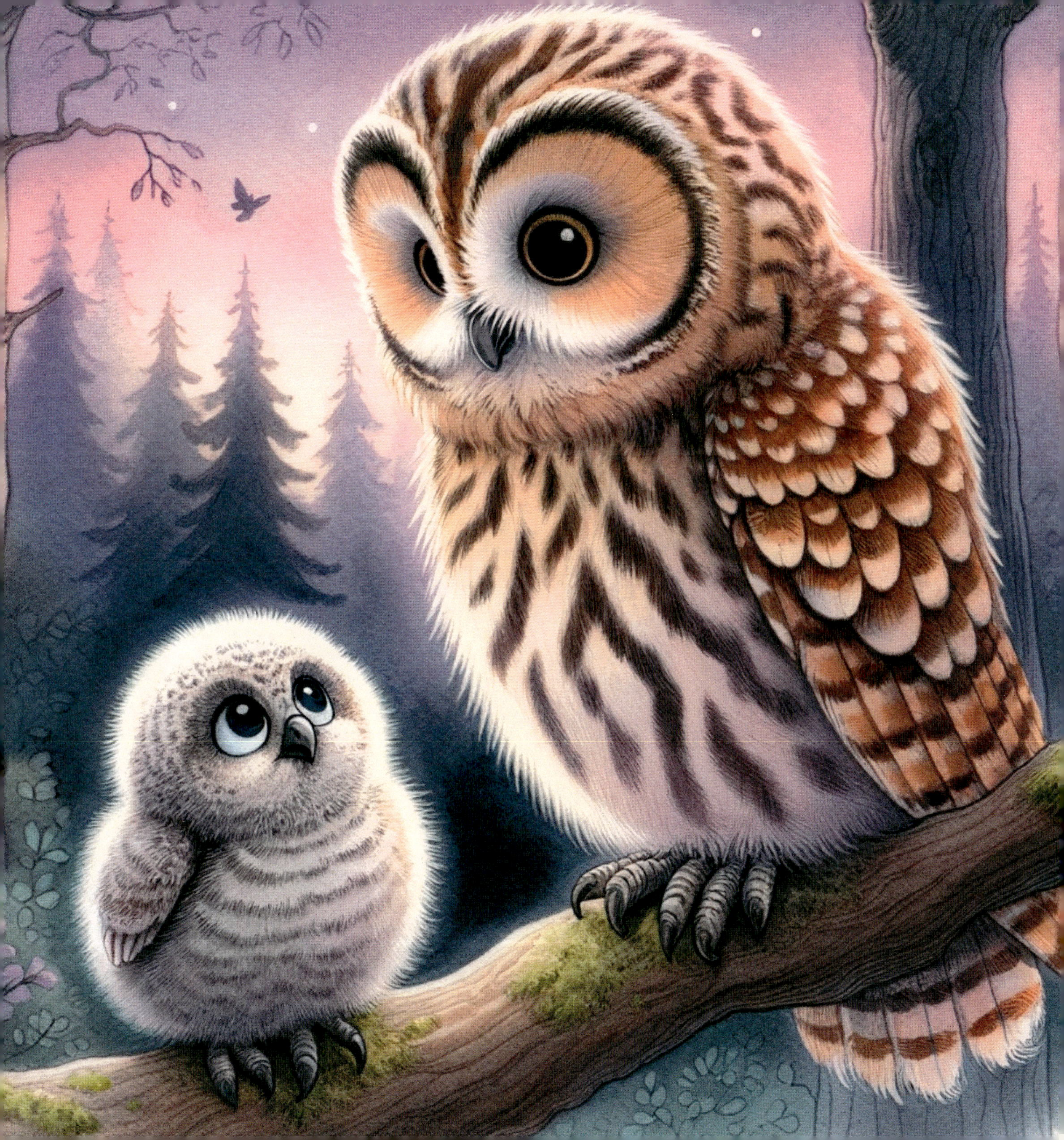

My little chick, feathers so sleek,
With your floppy wings, how unique!
Sliding on ice and diving so deep,
My darling penguin, to you my promise I'll always keep.

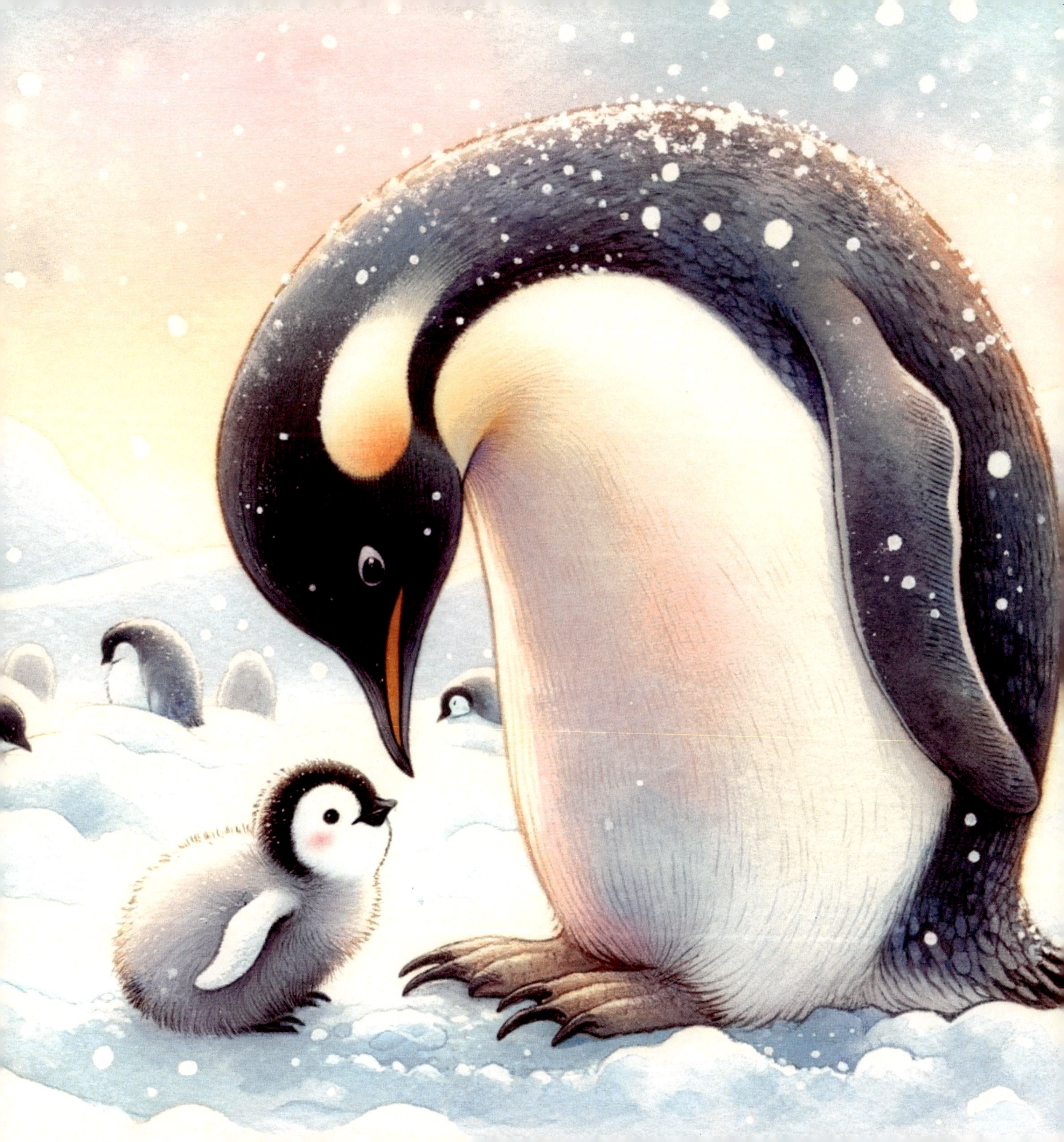

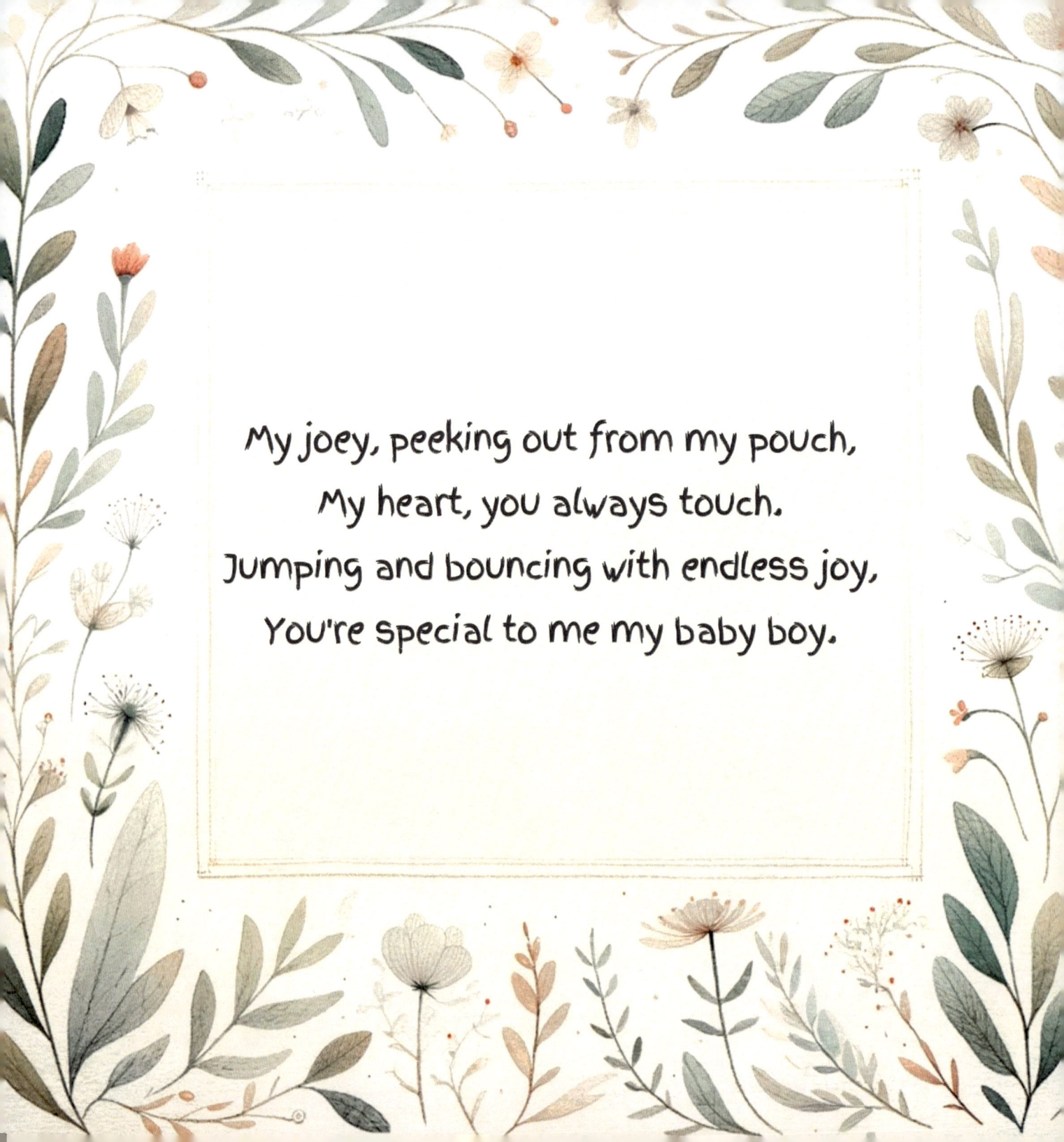

My joey, peeking out from my pouch,
My heart, you always touch.
Jumping and bouncing with endless joy,
You're special to me my baby boy.

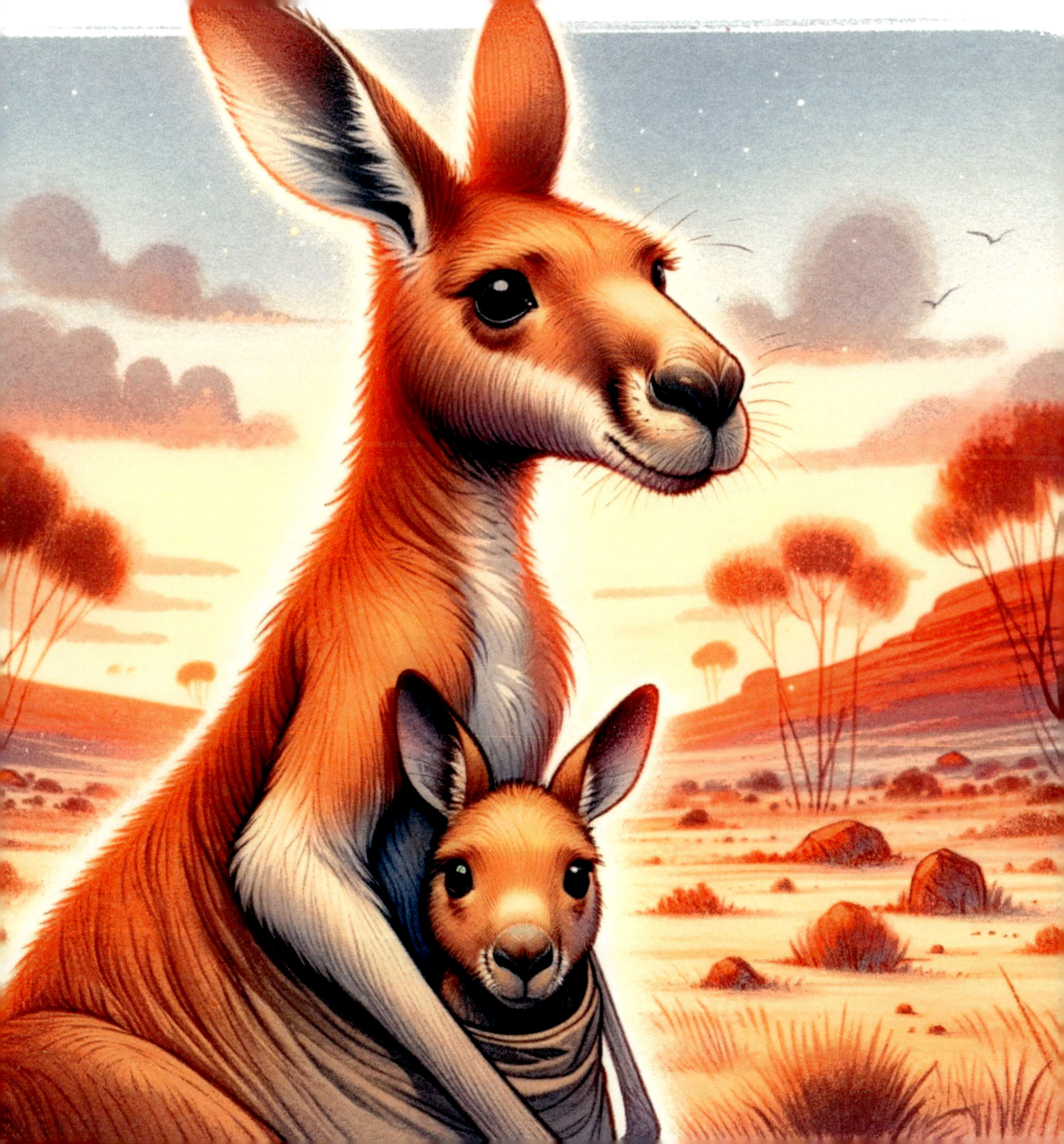

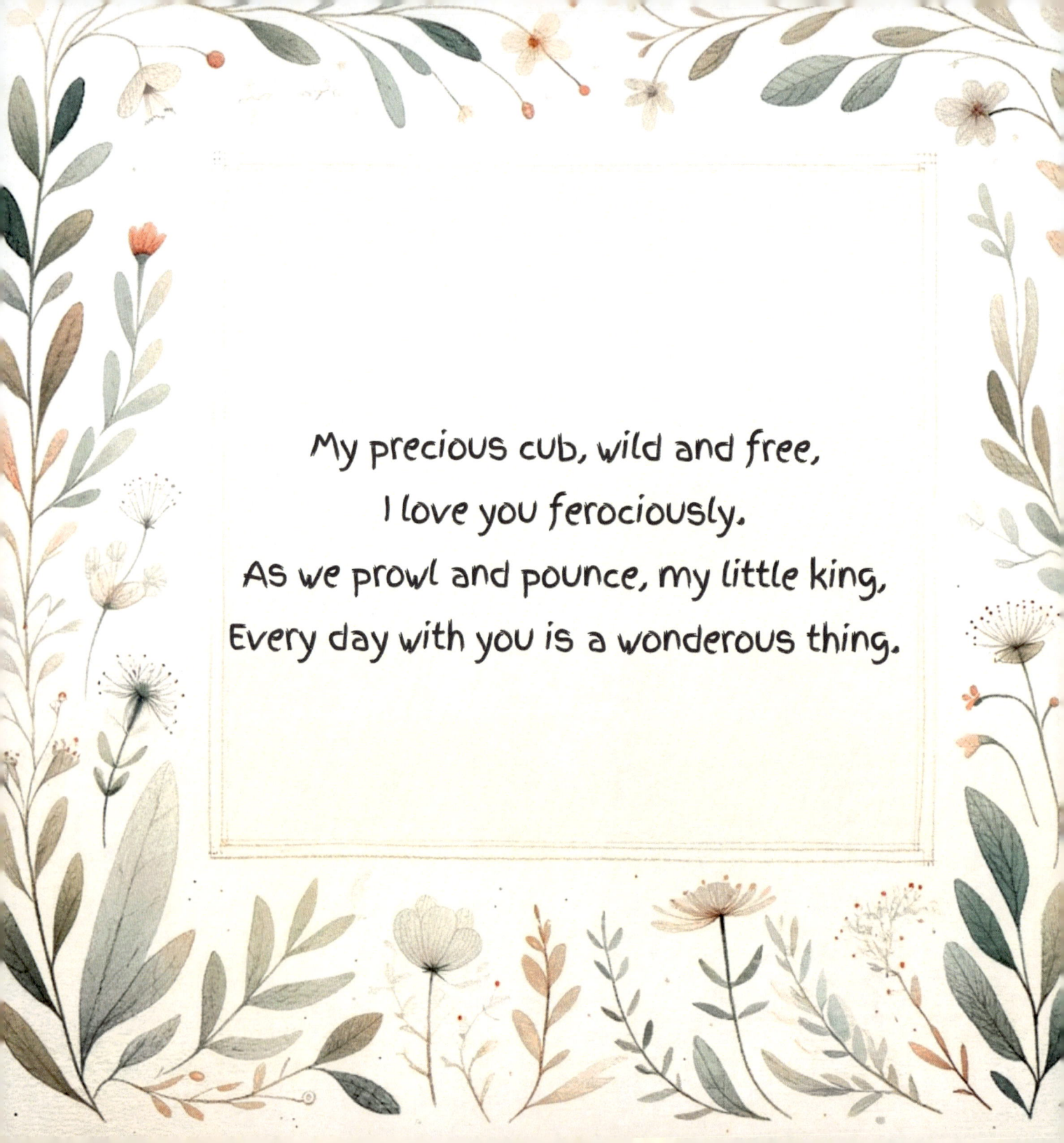

My precious cub, wild and free,
I love you ferociously.
As we prowl and pounce, my little king,
Every day with you is a wonderous thing.

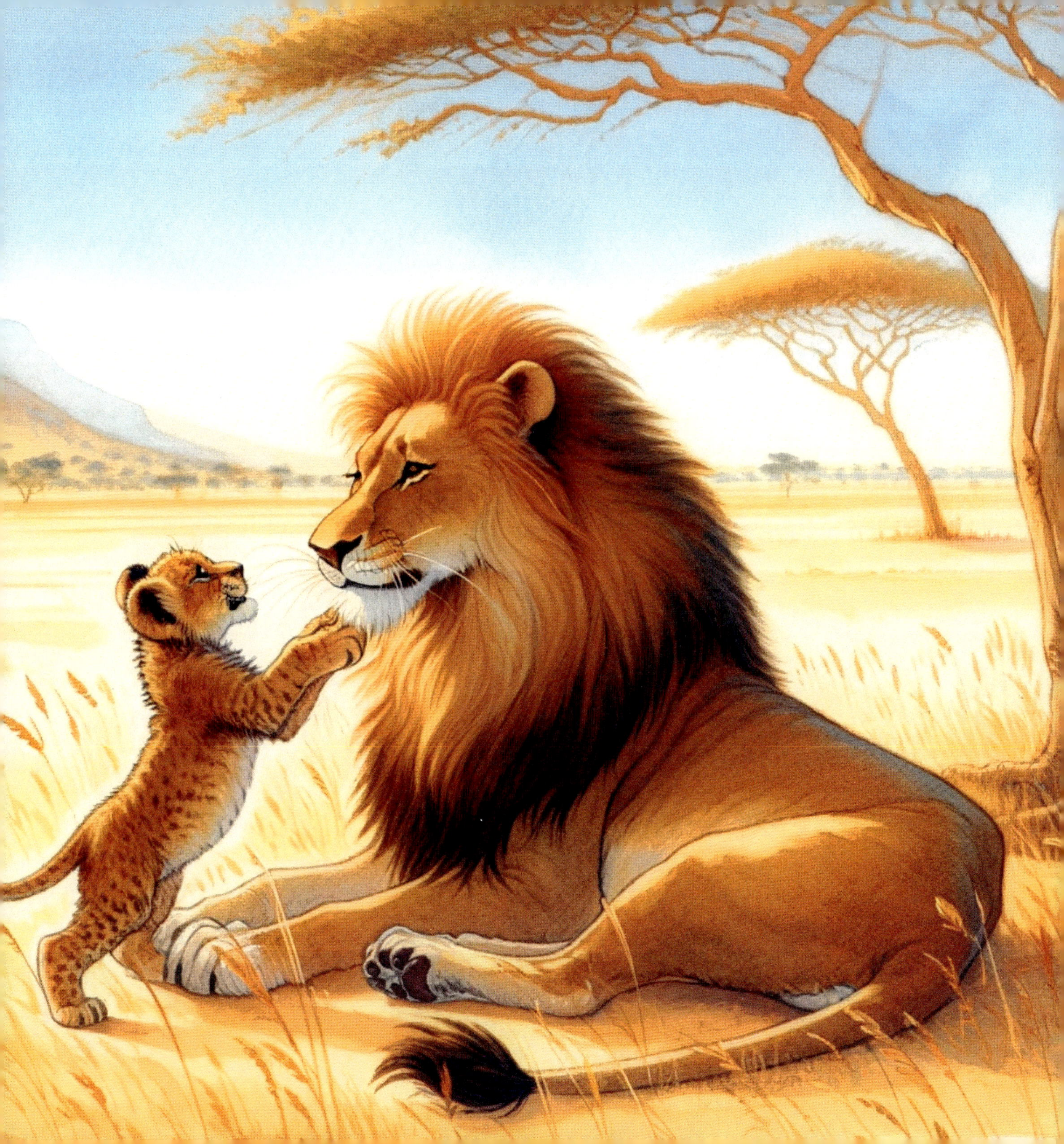

My little baby, let's leap and dive,
Doing flips, you're so alive!
Swimming together, playing all day,
Everything's better when you're here to stay.

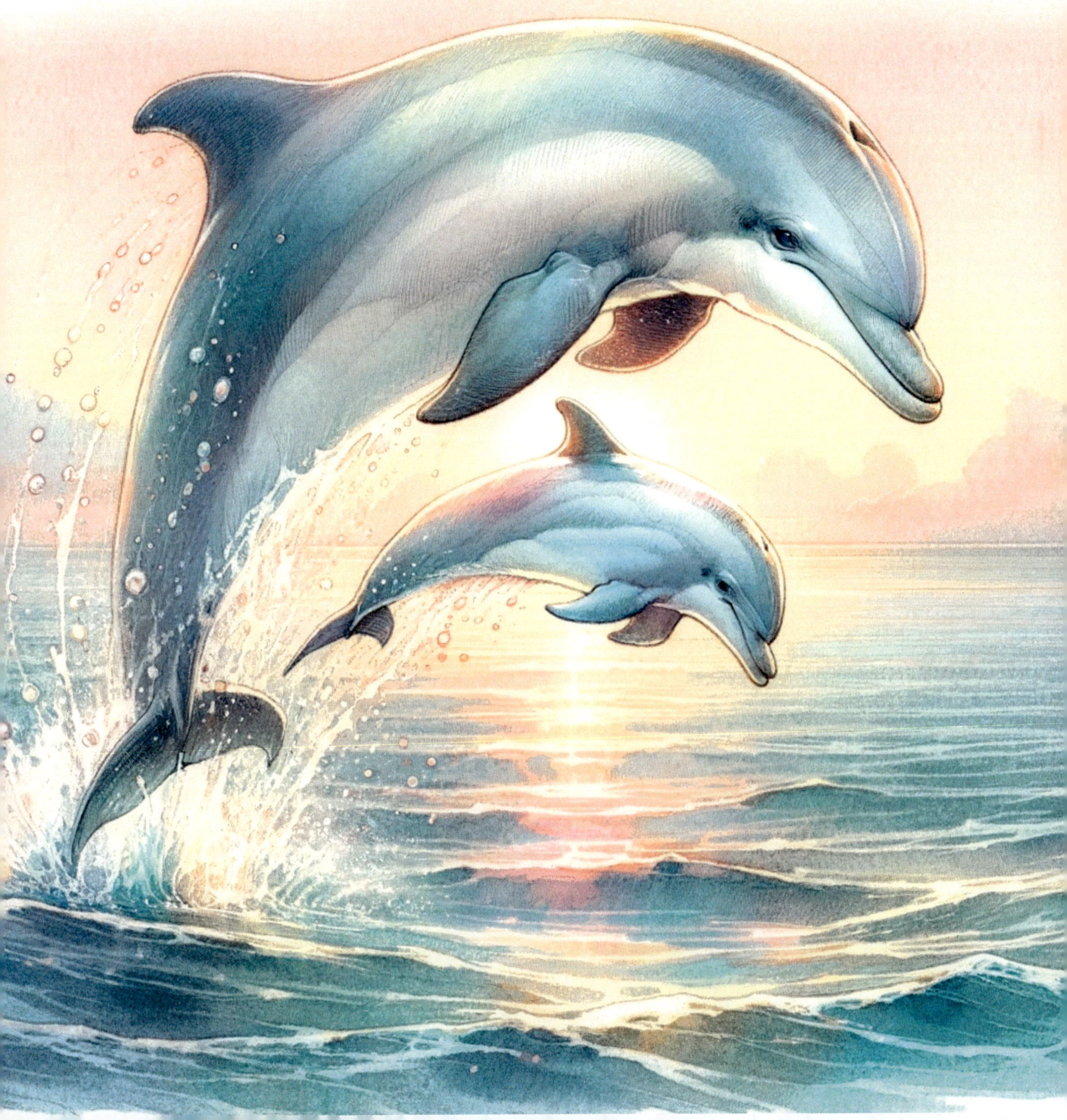

My baby squirrel, bushy and clever,
Of you, I'll be fond forever.
Climbing the tallest trees, quick as can be,
You'll always have a home here with me.

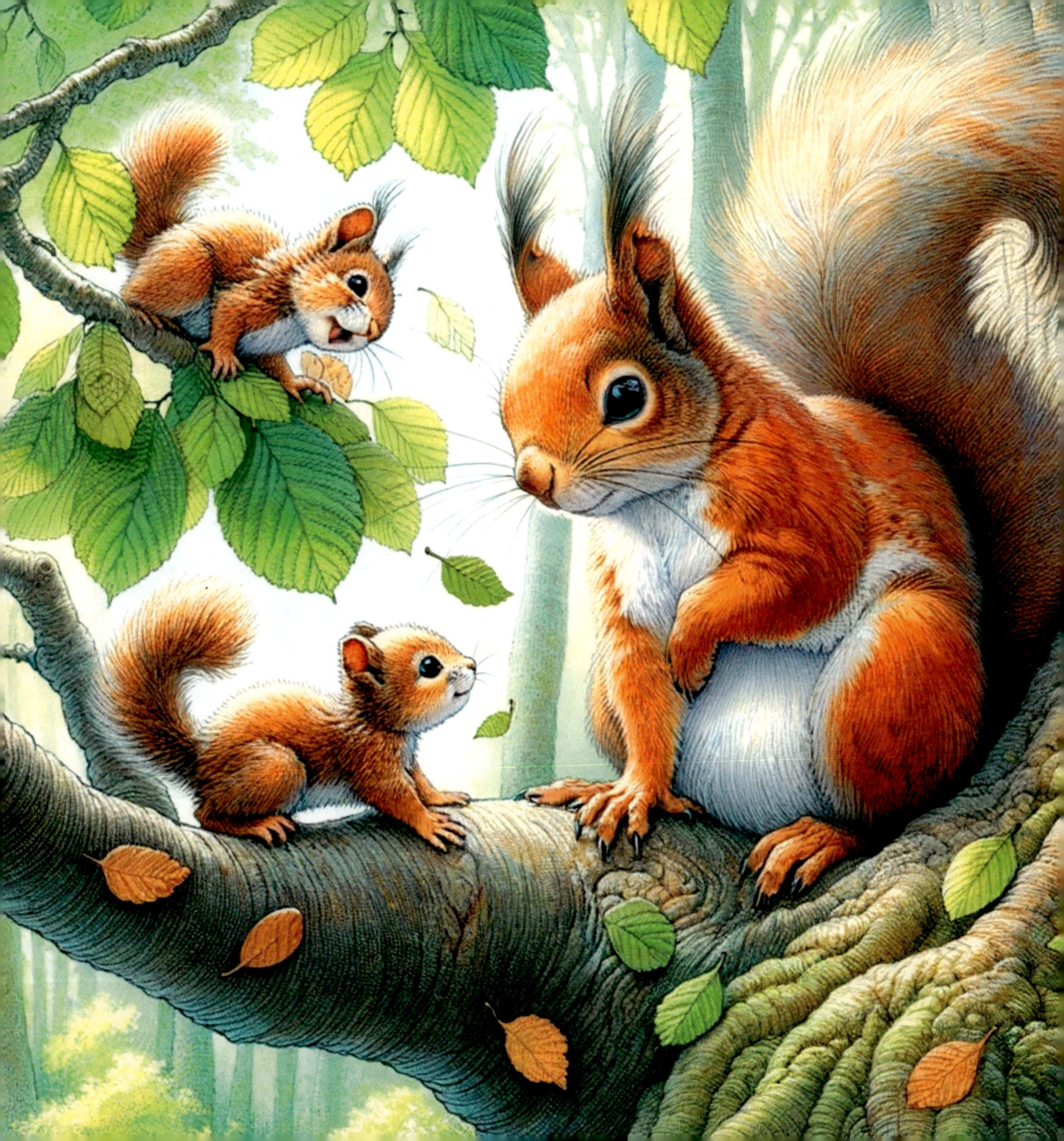

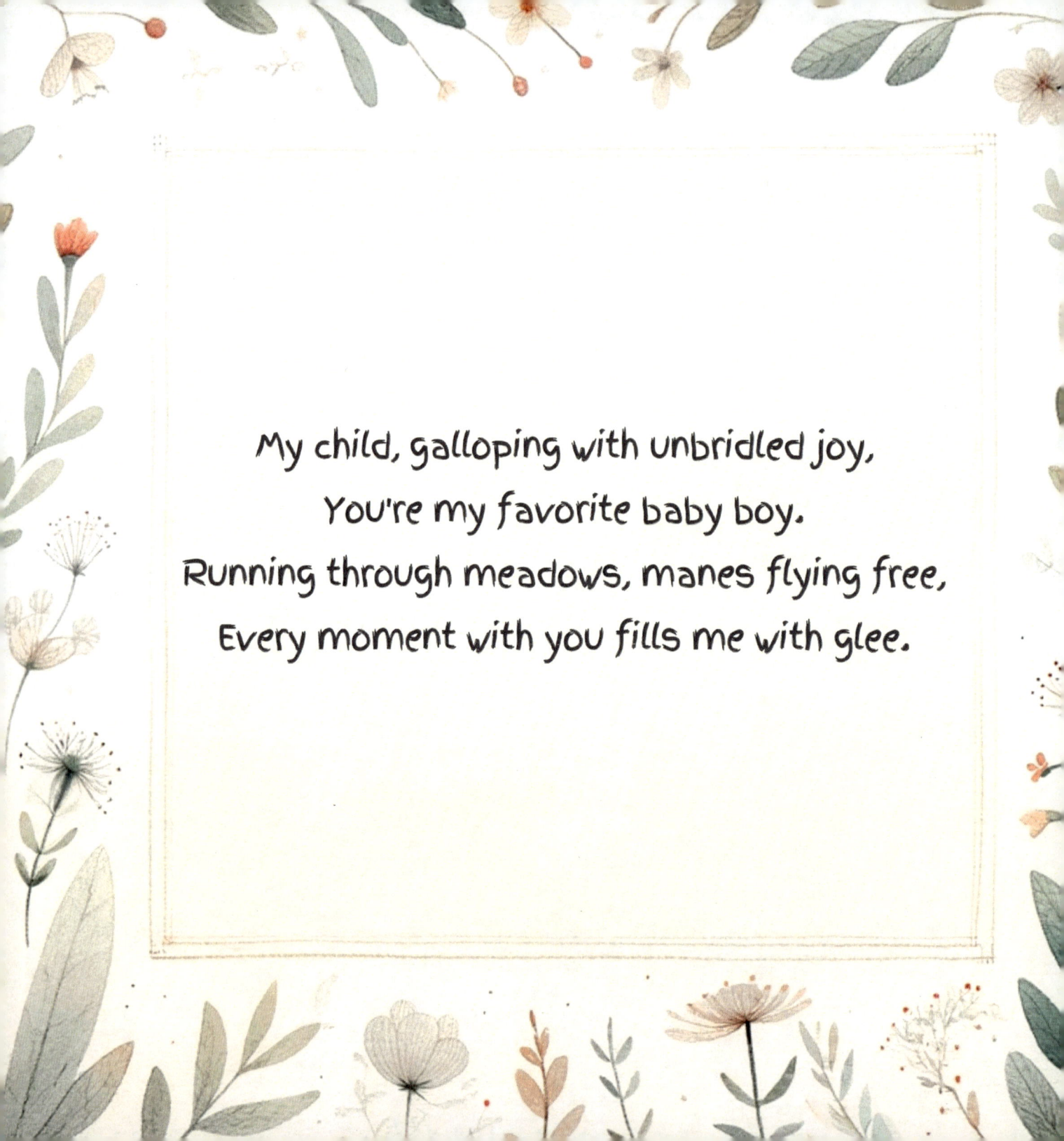

My child, galloping with unbridled joy,
You're my favorite baby boy.
Running through meadows, manes flying free,
Every moment with you fills me with glee.

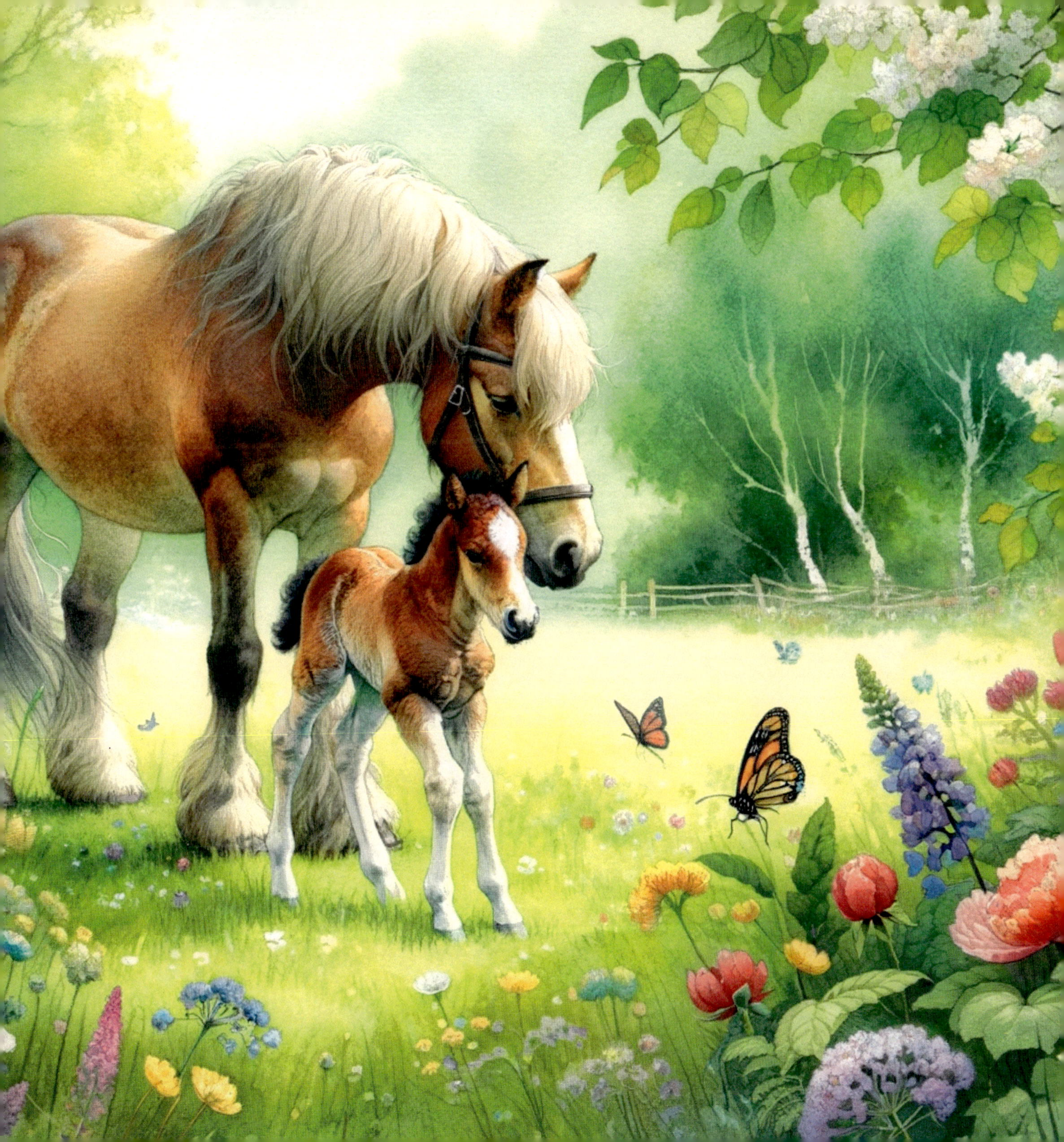

Dear Reader,

Thank you for choosing this book for your bedtime story. I hope you and your little ones enjoyed reading about how animals say "I Love You" to their babies.

As a self-published author, I rely on your feedback and support to help me reach more readers like you. If you liked this book, please consider leaving a review. Your honest opinion will help other customers find this book and enjoy it too.

Sincerely,
Emily Hartmann

Made in United States
Orlando, FL
16 September 2024

51578265R00015